Lobster Tales

Lobster Tales

recipes and recitations featuring the Maine attraction

Martha Griffin
The Kennebunkport Inn, Kennebunkport, Maine

Brooks MacDonald
Hurricane Restaurant, Ogunquit, Maine

with writings by
Valerie Tamis
Kennebunkport, Maine

Down East Books

To Rick and Louie, without whose love and support
this project would never have been possible.

Thank you,
Martha and Brooks

ISBN 0-89272-395-5

Book design by Darci Mehall, Aureo Design

Photographs copyright © Stock Food America

Printed and bound at Quebecor Printing Kingsport, Kingsport, TN

First printing November, 1995

DE 9 8 7 6 5 4 3 2 1

Down East Books
P.O. Box 679, Camden, Maine 04843
Book Orders: 1-800-766-1670

Contents

Acknowledgements

It is with extreme gratitude that we thank the following people for their hard work and tremendous support as we assembled this book. Thank you to Darci Mehall for showing us how to plan, design, and layout a cookbook and stay on schedule. To her husband Phil for all of his opinions, both legal and otherwise. Thank you Susie Porter for sending us in the right direction and introducing us to Denise Landis. Thanks Denise for all your recipe testing and editing. Jim will probably never want to eat lobster again. To Valerie Tamis, a heartfelt thank you for the Tales in *Tales.* You have a great way with words and now have the ability to be a good stern-person on any lobster boat as well. Thanks Bill Mathews for the background and boat rides, here's hoping all your traps fill daily. To Gerry and Mary, many thanks for all the tasting you did. Your input kept us on track from the start. Thank you Anne Speers for the one final read. Thanks so much to Peter and Susie Eising for the wonderful cover photos we used. Thanks to Scott Wilder for the wonderful Pizza recipe, and all your efforts at Hurricane. To Ken and Jeanne Young, thank you for sharing the *Ugly Anne's Lobster Stew* recipe. Thank you Paul Brick for understanding how much the project meant and keeping everything in line at Hurricane. A big thanks to Martin Crosby for the morning coffee conversations and the many lobster tales. To the staff at the Kennebunkport Inn and at Hurricane, thanks for allowing us the time that was needed to finish this undertaking. Thank you Kevin and Murph at Fosters Clambakes for the know-how in doing a true Down East bake. To each and every customer at both the Inn and at Hurricane, thank you for your kind words and tremendous encouragement.

Lobster Tales

A Lobster in Every Pot

Take two talented chefs who were born and raised along the rocky coast of Maine. Add a decade of experience running a downeast cooking school. Blend in flair and enthusiasm for the culinary arts, a life-long passion for lobster, and the mutual desire to create a unique cookbook together. The delectable result is *Lobster Tales.*

Martha Griffin is a graduate of Paris' La Varenne Ecole de Cuisine and London's Elizabeth Pomeroy School of Cookery. She and her husband own The Kennebunkport Inn where she is the supervisory chef. Brooks MacDonald and his wife own Hurricane, a restaurant in Ogunquit that has garnered five-star dining accolades in newspapers from Boston to Bar Harbor.

Selecting their "forty-five favorites" from hundreds of recipes they've used in their restaurants and cooking school over the years was not difficult. The inspiration was lobster. Martha and Brooks discovered that their most popular and requested recipes always featured lobster.

Lobster Tales demonstrates that there are countless and affordable ways to enjoy Maine's premier product, whether it takes the starring role in a cassoulet, gumbo, or fricassee. From lobster-stuffed artichoke appetizers, to traditional Maine chowder, to a full downeast lobster bake you can order directly from this book, *Lobster Tales* specializes in Maine cooking at its best.

If you're ready to indulge in a steamy fare . . . read on.

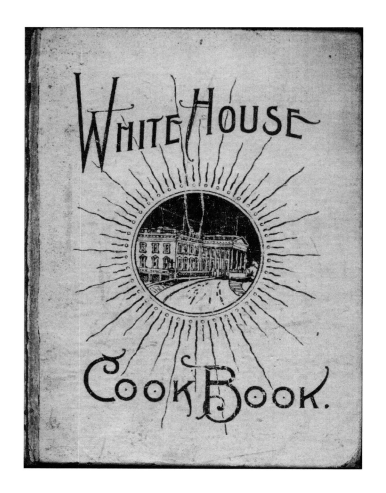

The White House Cook Book, published in 1904, proves that Maine's favorite crustacean was also a favorite of some of Washington's most famous. Recipes included Boiled Lobster, Scalloped Lobster, Deviled Lobster, Lobster Croquettes, Lobster Patties, and Lobster Á La Newburg (shown at right).

up the liver and all the rest of the terrapin into small pieces, adding the blood and juice that have flowed out in cutting up; add half a pint of water; sprinkle a little flour over them as you place them in the stewpan; let them stew slowly ten minutes, adding salt, black and cayenne pepper, and a very small blade of mace; then add a gill of the best brandy and half a pint of the very best sherry wine; let it simmer over a slow fire very gently. About ten minutes or so, before you are ready to dish them, add half a pint of rich cream, and half a pound of sweet butter, with flour, to prevent boiling; two or three minutes before taking them off the fire, peel the eggs carefully and throw them in whole. If there should be no eggs use the yolks of hens' eggs, hard boiled. This recipe is for four terrapins.

Renner's Hotel, Baltimore.

BOILED LOBSTER.

Put a handful of salt into a large kettle or pot of boiling water. When the water boils very hard put in the lobster, having first brushed it and tied the claws together with a bit of twine. Keep it boiling from twenty minutes to half an hour, in proportion to its size. If boiled too long the meat will be hard and stringy. When it is done take it out, lay it on its claws to drain, and then wipe it dry.

It is scarcely necessary to mention that the head of a lobster and what are called the lady fingers are not to be eaten.

Very large lobsters are not the best for boiling; the meat being coarse and tough. The male is best for boiling; the flesh is firmer and the shell a brighter red. It may readily be distinguished from the female; the tail is narrower, and the two uppermost fins within the tail are stiff and hard. Those of the hen lobster are not so, and the tail is broader.

Hen lobsters are preferred for sauce or salad, on account of their coral. The head and small claws are never used.

They should be alive and freshly caught when put into the kettle. After being cooked and cooled, split open the bod... crack the claws, to extract the meat. Care should be ... throat should be removed. The sand ... feathery, tough, gill-like particles fo... with the meat, as they are ... They are supposed to ... lobster.

... also be ...

SCALLOPED LOBSTER.

Butter a deep dish and cover the bottom with fine bread crumbs; put on this a layer of chopped lobster, with pepper and salt; so on, alternately, until the dish is filled, having crumbs on top. Put on bits of butter, moisten with milk and bake about twenty minutes.

DEVILED LOBSTER.

Take out all the meat from a boiled lobster, reserving the coral; season highly with mustard, cayenne, salt and some kind of table sauce; stew until well mixed and put it in a covered saucepan, with just enough hot water to keep from burning; rub the coral smooth, moistening with vinegar until it is thin enough to pour easily, then stir it into the sauce-pan. The dressing should be prepared before the meat is put on the fire, and which ought to boil but once before the coral is put in; stir in a heaping teaspoonful of butter, and when it boils again it is done and should be taken up at once, as too much cooking toughens the meat.

LOBSTER CROQUETTES.

Take any of the lobster remaining from table and pound it until the dark, light meat and coral are well mixed; season with pepper, salt and fine bread crumbs; put with it not quite as much pepper; add a little melted butter, about two tablespoonfuls if the bread is rather dry; form into egg-shaped or round balls; roll them in egg, then in fine crumbs, and fry in boiling lard.

LOBSTER PATTIES.

... one boiled lobster in small pieces; then take the small claws and ... put them in a suitable dish, and jam them to a paste with a ... Now add to them a ladleful of gravy or both, with a few ... set it over the fire and boil; strain it through a strainer, or ... thickness of a cream, and put half of it to your lobsters, and ... half to sauce them with after they are baked. Put to the ... ness of an egg of butter, a little pepper and salt; squeeze in ... these over the fire enough to melt the butter, set it to ... r patty pan or a plate or dish with good puff paste, then ... and cover it with a paste; bake it within three-quar... e you want it; when it is baked, cut up your cover, ... er half of your sauce above mentioned, with a little ... s of cream, and pour it over your patty, with a little

---

LOBSTER Á LA NEWBURG

Take one whole lobster, cut up in pieces about as large as a hickory nut. Put in the same pan with a piece of butter size of a walnut, and season with salt and pepper to taste, and thicken with heavy cream sauce; add the yolk of one egg and two oz. of sherry wine.

Cream sauce for above is made as follows: 1 oz. butter, melted in saucepan; 2 oz. flour, mixed with butter; thin down to proper consistency with boiling cream.

The American Lobster — The *Ultimate* White Meat

Product	Calories	Protein (grams)	Total Fat (grams)	Cholesterol (milligrams)
Lobster (boiled)	98	21	0.6	72
Chicken Breast (skinless, roasted)	165	31	3.6	85
Whole Egg (poached)	149	12	10.0	423
Beef (lean)	216	30	9.9	86

Nutrition information is based on 100 grams (3.5 oz.) of cooked edible product.

Nutrition information supplied in part by the New York Sea Grant Institute

Lobster is also high in:

- Amino acids
- Potassium and magnesium
- Vitamin B12, B6, B3 (niacin) and B2 (riboflavin)
- Calcium and phosphorous
- Iron, zinc, and vitamin A

Classification of Lobsters

• Chickens	1– 1-1/8 lb.
• Quarters	1-1/4 lb.
• Selects	1-1/2–1-3/4 lb.
• Deuces (2-pounders)	2–2-1/2 lb.
• Small Jumbos	2-1/2–3 lb.
• Jumbos	3 lb.- up

THE BOSTON HERALD, FRIDAY, AUGUST 4, 1995

Lobster roll feeds hundreds in Maine

By Paul Sullivan

Lobster is king in Island Falls, Maine, after a truck rollover there scattered 14,000 pounds' worth of free crustaceans on the side of the road.

"People were picking them up in big buckets, garbage pails, laundry bags — anything that would hold a lobster," said resident Patty Harkin. "Some were still in their crates and people just picked up the crate."

The god Neptune must have smiled on the residents of the town early Wednesday when a truck owned by Westmoreland Fisheries of Ca-Pele, New Brunswick, crashed through a guardrail and overturned at the junction of routes 95 and 159.

Maine State Police said the driver, Victor Doiron, 42, apparently fell asleep. He was treated at a local hospital for minor injuries and released.

With no nearby facilities available to handle the $55,000 worth of lobster, the owner of the truck asked police to have them distributed to the folks of the town in Northern Maine.

"It was first come, first serve, grab 'em and go," said one trooper. "I imagine by noon they were all gone. Word of mouth works pretty well."

It was not known if any of the lobsters attempted to hightail it to freedom.

Essentials

Lobster Lore

Maine lobster is considered a prized delicacy and holiday treat nowadays, but it wasn't always this high on the food chain.

In 1621, Miles Standish breakfasted on lobster at what one has to assume was the first Sunday Brunch in the Bay Colony and reportedly declared it "quite edible." His fellow settlers along the Atlantic coast, however, weren't quite as enthralled with the creepy-looking crustacean. When lobsters piled up on their local shores in the aftermath of a howling Nor'easter, they promptly dumped the critters in their newly spaded gardens as fertilizer. The extras were doled out to widows and orphans, or brought home to feed the servants.

Initially, the Staff was simply content to have a square meal. (The Colonial diet, remember, was slim-pickings.) But when the abundant and easily snared lobsters became their daily fare, the upstairs-downstairs crowd got a bit steamed up, if not boiling mad. "Not every night!" they begged with such fervor that Massachusetts passed a law making it illegal to serve lobster to servants more than twice a week.

During the Revolutionary War, the Minute Men used guile and wile to capture their British enemies, and labeled them "lobsterbacks" because of their bright red uniform jackets. The Brits kept a stiff upper lip about the name-calling, but eating New England jailhouse food was another matter. Once incarcerated, the prisoners were forced to dine on lobster every evening which soon had them longing for a plate of fish and chips. They staged food fights, and even threatened to riot. They tried anything to convince their American wardens that a daily lobster dinner was cruel and unjust punishment.

Back in the 1700s, the average lobster washing up on shore after a Nor'easter weighed between 5 and 15 pounds. Those 2 pounds or less were considered not worth keeping.

The nineteenth century marked a turning point in public appreciation of the Maine lobster. Heretofore, used primarily as bait to lure the more popular codfish, lobster suddenly became recognized as a dish fit for a queen . . . and an emperor. Napoleon is reputed to have savored a smashing victory by celebrating with Lobster Thermidor. Queen Victoria was so partial to lobster smothered in hollandaise sauce that she put it on the palace party menu.

Today Maine lobster is in huge demand worldwide, especially in the Far East. Since Asians like their lobsters alive and kicking, shipping methods are crucial and a new industry has arisen to meet that challenge. To ensure that lobsters survive the long haul from Maine waters to Seoul and Tokyo restaurants, entrepreneurs in Hawaii have created a mid-journey Club Crustacean, as it were. After the Maine lobsters arrive at the Honolulu airport, they are brought to special farms to recuperate. Beneath rustling palm trees, the lobsters shake off jet lag and the stress of travel by swimming in pools of chilly, just-like-home seawater for several days, after which they're reloaded in crates and sent to their rendezvous with destiny.

Two centuries ago Jonathan Swift wrote, "He was a bold man that first eat an oyster." Any Mainer worth his salt knows it took a very hungry man indeed to eat the first lobster. And once he did, the world was forever changed.

Hot Boiled Lobster

serves 6

INGREDIENTS

8 quarts sea water or salted tap water

6 1-1/2 pound lobsters

TO PREPARE

1. In a 12-quart pot, bring water to a rolling boil.

2. Remove elastic bands from lobsters and place lobsters head first into the boiling water.

3. Cover the pot with a lid and return to a boil.

4. Boil for 10 to 12 minutes, depending on the hardness of the shell. Lobsters should be done when the tentacle is easily snapped.

Lobster Butter

There are many uses for lobster butter. This is probably one of the most versatile recipes in the entire book. Throughout this book you will find many recipes in which the lobster butter can be used to enhance the flavor of a dish in place of regular butter. It is easy to make, stores well and can be kept frozen for up to 90 days in a properly sealed container.

INGREDIENTS

2 pounds unsalted butter

1 cup dry sherry

4 to 6 lobster bodies, rinsed and crushed

TO PREPARE

1. In a large heavy-bottomed pot add the butter, sherry, and lobster shells.
2. Simmer all ingredients on low heat for about one hour, being careful not to let butter burn, stirring occasionally.
3. Remove pot from heat, line strainer with cheese cloth and strain into bowl.
4. Let butter cool and store in one of the following ways:
   a. Pour into ice cube tray, wrap in plastic to seal tightly and freeze.
   b. Allow butter to cool in container until solid enough to handle. Discard liquid in bottom of container. Place softened butter on plastic wrap, roll into one inch log form and seal tightly and freeze.
   c. Keep in plastic container in refrigerator for up to three weeks.

DID YOU KNOW?

Lobster butter is great on grilled fresh fish.

Lobster butter is excellent for sauteing shrimp, scallops, or fish.

It is also great melted and served with steamers or mussels.

For an unusual twist serve lobster butter with fresh corn on the cob.

Lobster Oil

makes 2 cups

INGREDIENTS

6 lobster bodies, cleaned, rinsed, and crushed

2 cups olive oil

TO PREPARE

1. Bring lobsters bodies and oil to a boil in a heavy-bottomed pan.

2. Lower heat and simmer for 2 hours.

3. Strain through cheese cloth and store in a tightly sealed glass bottle for up to 30 days.

Lobster Stock

makes about 2 quarts

INGREDIENTS

5 lobster bodies, cleaned and chopped

2 tablespoons olive oil or Lobster Oil (see page 16)

2 cups chardonnay wine

1/2 cup brandy

2 tablespoons unsalted butter

1 celery rib, chopped

1 small onion, chopped

2 leeks, white part only, chopped

1 fennel bulb, chopped

4 unpeeled cloves garlic

2 sprigs parsley

1 51-ounce can clam juice

1 tablespoon tomato paste

4 plum tomatoes, chopped

2 sprigs thyme

TO PREPARE

1. Preheat oven to 375 degrees.

2. Place lobster bodies in a roasting pan and sprinkle with oil. Roast for 20 to 25 minutes, stirring once.

3. Set the roasting pan on a burner on high heat. Pour chardonnay and brandy slowly over the bodies, and scrape the bottom of the pan well.

4. In a large pot over high heat melt the butter and add the celery, onion, leeks, fennel, and garlic. Cook until soft and lightly browned, about 10 minutes.

5. Add the roasted lobster bodies with their liquid, and cook until all the liquid has evaporated. Add the tomato paste, plum tomatoes, thyme, parsley, clam juice and two quarts of water.

6. Bring to a simmer. Skim the stock and reduce the heat to low. Simmer, partially covered, for 1-1/2 hours.

7. Allow stock to cool. Strain through a fine sieve lined with cheesecloth. Refrigerate or freeze until ready for use.

How to Eat (Pick) a Lobster

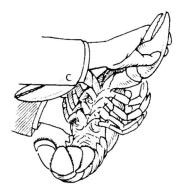

1. twist off the claws

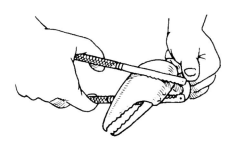

2. crack each claw with a nutcracker, pliers, knife, hammer, or anything handy

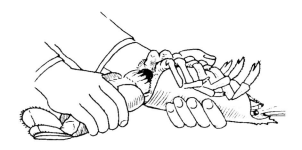

3. separate the tailpiece from the body by arching the back until it cracks

4. bend back and break the flippers off the tailpiece

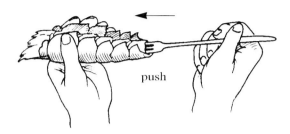

push

5. insert a fork where the flippers broke off and push

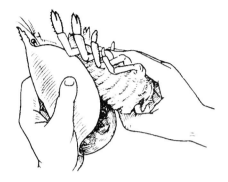

6. unhinge the back from the body — don't overlook the "tomalley" or liver of the lobster which turns green when cooked and is considered a delicacy

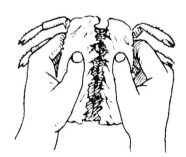

7. open the remaining part of the body by cracking apart sideways — there is good meat in this section, too

8. break off the small claws and suck the meat out

Small Plates

Lobster
Nuggets

American lobster troll the 1300-mile stretch of the Atlantic Ocean between Cape Hatteras and Labrador, but the choicest specimens thrive along the rocky coast of Maine. They are the Northeast's premier and most valuable fishery product. Last year's catch in Maine's ideal 49-degrees off-shore waters exceeded 38 million pounds and accounted for more than half of all lobsters caught in the United States. Lobster is such a downeast totem, it's even featured on the Maine license plate.

Prestige and acclaim notwithstanding, this cranky oceanic vagabond wouldn't stand a chance of winning the Congeniality Award at a Crustacean Pageant. For sure, members of its own species wouldn't vote for him. Snoopy, shy and a tad on the surly side, the Maine lobster passes most evenings slinking around the ocean bottom looking for a wimpier version of itself to dine on. Like us, it appreciates fresh cod, clams and crabmeat, but has a keener predilection for succulent lobster meat.

If they're lucky (Lobster-Speak for: I'm not going NEAR that trap) or don't bump into a larger predator, lobsters generally live about 15 years. Scientists have no absolute verification or method of gauging a lobster's age, but they estimate that a Nova Scotia specimen caught in 1977, weighing 44-1/2 pounds and measuring a bodacious 42 inches from tip to tail, was probably 100 years old. (Caveat to swimmers: He was rare.)

As was the blue specimen caught several decades off Kennebunkport, which was considered a "one in a million" catch. Though lobsters can also be red, yellow, even half one color and half another, they're predominantly green in hue.

Most Maine lobsters are right-handed, as indicated by their larger "crusher" claw. But if that chopper gets ripped off in a skirmish or stuck in a rocky crevice, the lobster reveals its uncanny ambidexterity by turning into a southpaw while the right claw regenerates, a process that can take two or three years.

Encased in bulky suits of armor, Maine lobsters pass the hours eating, reproducing, hiding and molting (shedding their shells). During their first seven years, they might molt 25 times (usually emerging 40% heavier and 15% larger), after which they shed once annually. They prefer to molt during the summer months when Maine's water temperatures are less bracing. It takes nearly two weeks for their new paper-thin shells to toughen, and a full six months before they are truly hard. The abundance of these soft-shell lobsters (called "shedders") during July and August lightens a lobsterman's daily haul, but the scarcity of the more popular hard-shell lobsters escalates the price. Several years ago in July, when the cost of lobster skyrocketed in Maine, a local opined, "Guess I'll have to settle for steak." Another rejoined, "And when the price comes down, I'd like to give ya some."

From a dietary perspective, Maine lobster has proven to be healthy for the heart. Recent studies reveal that a 3-1/2 ounce serving is lower in saturated fat, cholesterol and calories than a comparable serving of skinless turkey or chicken. Replacing hot melted butter with lemon juice for dipping purposes eliminates even more calories and fat. In Maine it's truly "the ultimate white meat."

Lobster meat contains omega-3 fatty acids, the substances that seem to reduce hardening of the arteries and decrease the risk of heart disease.

Deviled Lobster Cakes

with fresh tomato and cilantro salsa

serves 8

INGREDIENTS

1 tablespoon diced green pepper

1 small onion, diced

1 tablespoon diced red bell pepper

2 tablespoons diced celery

1 teaspoon black pepper

1/2 teaspoon salt

4 drops (or to taste) Tabasco Sauce

4 cups fresh bread crumbs (don't use packaged)

1 pound fresh picked lobster meat

1 egg

1/2 cup butter or Lobster Butter (see page 15), melted

2 tablespoons olive oil or Lobster Oil (see page 16)

8 sprigs of cilantro, for garnish

2 lemons, quartered, for garnish

Fresh Tomato and Cilantro Salsa (recipe follows)

TO PREPARE

1. Saute vegetables until onions are transparent.

2. Add seasonings and mix in bread crumbs, lobster meat, egg, and butter.

3. Form sixteen patties (about 1 ounce each) and refrigerate until ready for use. This may be done one day in advance.

4. Preheat oven to 400 degrees.

5. Rub a sheet pan with lobster or olive oil and place cakes so that they are not touching. Bake for 8 minutes and remove from oven and turn cakes over and continue to bake for 4 more minutes.

6. Remove from oven and garnish with fresh cilantro sprigs and lemon wedges. Serve with Fresh Tomato and Cilantro Salsa.

Fresh Tomato and Cilantro Salsa

yield 1-1/2 cups

INGREDIENTS

3/4 cup plum tomatoes, diced

1 tablespoon minced fresh cilantro

2 tablespoons diced celery

1/4 cup diced red onion

2 tablespoons diced green pepper

2 scallions (white and green), sliced

1/4 teaspoon salt

1/4 teaspoon prepared horseradish

1/4 teaspoon white vinegar

1 teaspoon granulated sugar

1 teaspoon worcestershire sauce

1 jalapeño pepper, seeded and finely diced

TO PREPARE

Mix all ingredients and refrigerate over night in a non-metallic container to mull flavors.

Lobster Cocktail

serves 4

INGREDIENTS

2 1-1/2 pound lobsters

4 tablespoons Cocktail Sauce (recipe below)

4 lettuce leaves

TO PREPARE

1. Boil lobsters according to the recipe on page 14, rinse under cold water and refrigerate until well chilled.
2. Remove lobsters from refrigerator and split lengthwise. Remove sac and stomach and rinse under cold water.
3. Remove meat from claws, knuckles, and tail and cut into bite-sized pieces.
4. Mix lobster meat with 4 tablespoons of the cocktail sauce. Line body cavities with lettuce and divide meat among each half and serve on a chilled plate.

Cocktail Sauce

INGREDIENTS

1 cup ketchup or chili sauce

2 tablespoons horseradish (or to taste)

1/2 teaspoon worcestershire sauce

1 teaspoon fresh squeezed lemon juice

salt and pepper

TO PREPARE

Combine all ingredients and mix well. Store in non-metallic container until ready for use.

Lobster Salsa

serves 6

INGREDIENTS

1/2 green pepper, diced

1 yellow pepper, diced

1 orange pepper, diced

2 jalapeño peppers, seeded and diced

4 medium tomatoes, diced

1/2 medium red onion, diced

6 scallions, sliced

juice of one lime

1 teaspoon balsamic vinegar

2 tablespoons extra virgin olive oil

1 tablespoon chopped fresh cilantro

1 teaspoon minced fresh garlic

1 tablespoon sugar

1/2 teaspoon chili powder

1/2 teaspoon oregano

1/4 teaspoon salt

5 twists of peppermill

1/2 pound fresh picked lobster meat, cut into bite-sized pieces

TO PREPARE

1. In a non-metallic bowl, mix all ingredients except lobster and refrigerate overnight or at least 6 hours.

2. Add 1/2 pound of fresh picked lobster meat to the salsa. Toss well.

DID YOU KNOW?

Lobster salsa is great as a dip with warmed tortilla chips.

It's a great accompaniment for grilled tuna, halibut, salmon, or swordfish.

It adds a new twist to a Mexican Omelette.

Lobster Pizza

tops 1 7-inch pizza

INGREDIENTS

1 uncooked pizza shell (your favorite, or see next page)

1/2 cup Roasted Garlic Pesto (see page 32)

4 tablespoons chevre cheese

1 red bell pepper, roasted, peeled, seeded, and cut julienne

1/4 cup mozzarella cheese, shredded

1 cup (2 ounces) fresh picked lobster meat

TO PREPARE

1. Preheat oven to 350 degrees.

2. Place the dough on a pizza stone or a pizza peel.

3. Place the peppers around the pizza and top with the chevre and lobster meat. Sprinkle evenly with mozzarella.

4. Bake for 20 to 25 minutes, or until the cheese is melted and lightly browned.

Pizza Dough

INGREDIENTS

3 cups all-purpose flour

1 teaspoon salt

1 tablespoon honey

2 tablespoons olive oil

3/4 cup cool water

1/4 ounce package dry yeast

1/4 cup warm water

TO PREPARE

1. Place the flour in the bowl of a food processor.

2. In a small bowl or measuring cup combine the salt, honey, olive oil, and cool water. Mix well.

3. Dissolve the yeast in the warm water and set aside for 10 minutes.

4. In food processor fitted with the knife blade, while processor is running, slowly pour the salt and honey mixture through the feed tube. When all the liquid has been added, pour in the yeast mixture. Process until the dough forms a ball. If it seems too sticky, add a very small amount of flour.

5. Transfer the dough to a lightly floured surface. Knead for about 10 minutes, or until the dough is smooth and elastic. Place the dough in a lightly oiled bowl, and allow to rest, covered, for 30 minutes.

6. Divide the dough into 3 equal parts and roll each into a small ball. Place on a flat dish, cover with a damp towel, and refrigerate up to 3 hours.

7. One hour before baking, remove the dough from the refrigerator and allow to come to room temperature. On a lightly floured work surface, roll a ball of dough into a circle and flatten into desired thickness. Repeat with the two other dough balls.

Roasted Garlic Pesto

makes about 1-1/2 cups

INGREDIENTS

1 large garlic bulb

1/2 cup olive oil (not extra virgin) or salad oil

4 ounces pine nuts

6 ounces freshly grated parmesan cheese

2 firmly packed cups fresh basil leaves

TO PREPARE

1. Preheat oven to 350 degrees. Slice off the top of the garlic bulb, rub it with oil, and wrap in foil. Roast for 45 minutes to an hour, until soft. Remove from oven and set aside.

2. Place the pine nuts and half the parmesan cheese in a food processor fitted with the knife blade and pulse 3 or 4 times.

3. Remove the roasted garlic from the foil and squeeze the pulp from the cloves into the processor bowl. Add some of the basil leaves and pulse 3 or 4 more times. Repeat until all of the basil has been used.

4. Add the remaining parmesan cheese and the rest of the oil and pulse 3 or 4 more times.

Lobster Stuffed Artichoke Bottoms with Hollandaise Mousseline

serves 4

INGREDIENTS

8 artichoke bottoms

4 ounces fresh picked lobster meat, cut into bite-sized pieces

HOLLANDAISE MOUSSELINE

3 egg yolks

1 tablespoon water

1/2 pound butter, melted

3 tablespoons fresh lemon juice

salt and pepper to taste

3 tablespoons heavy cream, whipped

TO PREPARE THE MOUSSELINE

1. In a food processor fitted with the knife blade, beat the egg yolks and water for 30 seconds. With the machine running, add the melted butter in a slow steady stream.
2. Add the lemon juice, salt and pepper and process just to blend.
3. Remove from the processor bowl and fold in the whipped cream.

TO PREPARE THE ARTICHOKES

1. Preheat oven to 400 degrees.
2. Place artichoke bottoms filled with 1/2 ounce of lobster meat in a shallow baking dish. Artichokes should fill the dish, but not be packed too tightly.
3. Pour sauce over the lobster-stuffed artichoke bottoms and bake in oven for 5 minutes.
4. Turn oven to broiler setting and brown tops of artichokes.

Lobster Paté

yields 2 cups

INGREDIENTS

1/2 cup shelled pistachio nuts

4 ounces fresh sole or any flat fish, cut into 1 inch pieces

4 tablespoons Lobster Butter (see page 15), or unsalted butter

1-1/2 cups fresh picked lobster meat

1/2 teaspoon salt

1 tablespoon brandy

TO PREPARE

1. Roast nuts in a 200 degree oven for 10 minutes so as to loosen the skin when rubbed with a towel. Remove as much skin as possible, chop into coarse pieces, and set aside.

2. Saute sole in Lobster Butter over low heat for 3 or 4 minutes until fish is just opaque. Transfer the mixture to the bowl of a food processor with the knife blade attached.

3. Add half of the lobster meat to the bowl and process until the mixture is smooth and well blended. Add the brandy, salt and the pistachios and stir well.

4. Coarsely chop the remaining lobster meat and stir it into the mixture. Place in a decorative crock or bowl and refrigerate for at least 2 hours. Bring to room temperature before serving.

Chilled Lobster Mousse

INGREDIENTS

1 tablespoon unflavored gelatin

1/4 cup cold water

3/4 cup mayonnaise

3 tablespoons lemon juice

1/2 teaspoon dried tarragon

1 cup celery, diced

1/4 cup onion, diced

1-1/2 cups fresh picked lobster meat, diced

1/3 cup heavy cream, whipped

salt and pepper to taste

TO PREPARE

1. Soften the gelatin in the cold water, place over simmering water and stir until it has been completely dissolved.

2. Add the gelatin and the lemon juice to the mayonnaise and stir well.

3. In the bowl of a food processor with the knife blade attached, add the tarragon, celery, onion, and lobster meat and process to a smooth consistency.

4. Fold the mayonnaise mixture into the lobster, fold the whipped cream into that and season with salt and pepper.

5. Turn the mixture into your favorite mold or loaf pan and refrigerate until firm.

Lobster & Mushroom Frittata

serves 4

INGREDIENTS

1/2 cup mushrooms, sliced

1 cup fresh picked lobster meat

3 tablespoons butter

4 eggs, beaten

3 tablespoons heavy cream

salt and pepper to taste

pinch of basil

2 teaspoons parsley, chopped

3 tablespoons parmesan cheese, grated

1 tablespoons olive oil

1/2 teaspoon lemon juice

4 ounces gruyere cheese, cubed

TO PREPARE

1. Preheat oven to 400 degrees.

2. Saute the mushrooms and lobster meat in 2 tablespoons of butter and set aside.

3. Mix the eggs, cream, salt, pepper, basil, parsley and 1 tablespoon of parmesan cheese.

4. Heat the olive oil and 1 tablespoon of butter in an oven-proof heavy skillet until hot. Pour the egg mixture into the skillet, reduce the heat and cook on very low heat until the eggs start to set on top. Remove from heat.

5. Top the eggs with the mushrooms, lobster meat, the remaining parmesan cheese, lemon juice, and mozzarella.

6. Place skillet in the oven and bake until cheese has melted.

Chilled Lobster Pasta with Cucumbers & Goat Cheese

serves 6

INGREDIENTS

1/2 cup olive oil

2 tablespoons fresh squeezed lemon juice

2 cloves garlic, minced

1/4 cup fresh basil, chopped

salt and fresh ground pepper to taste

1 pound small pasta shells

1 red pepper, diced

1 yellow pepper, diced

1 cucumber, peeled, halved, seeded, and sliced

1 red onion, halved and sliced thin

3 plum tomatoes, chopped

1/4 cup fresh parsley, chopped

1/2 pound goat cheese, crumbled

1/2 pound fresh picked lobster meat, chopped

TO PREPARE

1. Combine olive oil, lemon juice, garlic, basil, salt and pepper and reserve.
2. Cook shells according to the directions on the package, drain and reserve.
3. Add peppers, cucumber, onion, tomatoes, parsley, goat cheese, and lobster meat to the pasta and toss well.
4. Add the dressing. Toss well and refrigerate for at least 2 hours or until ready for use.

Lobster Quiche with Mascarpone Cheese

serves 8

INGREDIENTS

1 11" pie crust, your favorite recipe (or see next page)

2-1/2 cups heavy cream

4 large eggs

1 cup mascarpone cheese

1/4 teaspoon salt

4 twists of peppermill

1 tablespoon dry sherry

8 ounces fresh picked lobster meat, cut into bite-sized pieces

2 teaspoons garlic chives, snipped

TO PREPARE

1. Preheat oven to 400 degrees.

2. Whisk together cream, eggs, cheese, salt, pepper, and sherry.

3. Spread lobster meat evenly on the bottom of the pie shell and sprinkle with the chives.

4. Slowly pour the cream mixture into the pie shell.

5. Bake at 400 degrees for 15 minutes, lower the heat to 325 degrees and continue to bake for 35 minutes or until a knife inserted will come out clean.

6. Remove from oven and allow it to sit for at least 10 minutes before serving.

PASTRY FOR QUICHE

yield: one 11-inch crust

1-1/2 cups flour

pinch of salt

8 tablespoons unsalted butter, cut into small pieces

2 to 3 tablespoons ice water

1. Put all ingredients except water in the bowl of a food processor fitted with the knife blade. Process for 4 seconds to blend in the butter.
2. Add the water just until the pastry pulls away from the sides of the bowl.
3. Flour a flat surface. Roll the dough with a rolling pin into a circle about 13 inches in diameter.
4. Put the dough into a 11-inch deep-dish pie pan and work the dough into the pan carefully. Crimp the edges of the pie shell.
5. Refrigerate the pie shell for 10 to 15 minutes.

Lobster Potatoes Anna

serves 4

INGREDIENTS

1-1/2 pounds russet potatoes

1 tablespoon olive oil

1/2 pound fresh picked lobster meat, coarsely chopped

6 ounces butter or Lobster Butter (see page 15), melted

1 tablespoon snipped fresh chives

TO PREPARE

1. Preheat oven to 450 degrees.

2. Peel potatoes and wipe clean. (Do not wash with water as you don't want to lose any of their starch.)

3. Slice the potatoes to 1/8-inch thickness.

4. In a well-oiled 9-inch oven-proof saute pan, arrange a layer of potatoes, making sure that they overlap. Sprinkle with a scant cup of lobster meat, 1/4 cup of melted butter, and 1-1/2 teaspoons chives. Make a second layer the same as the first. Top with a third layer of potatoes and 1/4 cup of butter.

5. Cover potatoes with a double layer of well-buttered foil and weight with a heavy pan.

6. Cook potatoes over moderate heat on stove top until the butter starts to sizzle.

7. Remove heavy pan and place potatoes into a hot (450 degree) oven and cook for 20 minutes.

8. Weight the potatoes again and continue to cook for another 30 minutes or until they are tender.

9. Remove from oven and drain excess butter. Let sit for a few minutes and turn onto a serving platter and cut into wedges to serve.

Lobster Hash

serves 4

INGREDIENTS

6 scallions, sliced

1 cup peeled and diced carrots, cooked until just tender

1 cup peeled and diced turnips, cooked until just tender

2 cups peeled and diced potatoes, cooked until just tender

1 teaspoon olive oil

1 teaspoon finely chopped fresh chives

1 teaspoon finely chopped fresh thyme

3 tablespoons Lobster Oil (see page 16)

1/4 cup heavy cream

8 ounces fresh picked lobster meat, cut into bite-sized pieces

TO PREPARE

1. Saute scallions, carrots, turnips, and potatoes in olive oil in a heavy-bottomed pan until vegetables start to brown.

2. Add the herbs and the lobster oil and continue to cook until vegetables are browned, 5 to 10 minutes over medium heat.

3. Add the 1/4 cup of heavy cream and the lobster meat and continue to cook until the cream has been absorbed. Allow the hash to brown between stirrings.

4. Divide hash on 4 plates and serve with poached eggs.

Soups & Salads

Lobstermen

Through mists thick as smoke, in pelting rain or sudden snow squalls, the downeast lobsterman makes his rounds along the coastal waters of the Gulf of Maine. He's both a marine engineer and a versatile tinker, an adventurous sea rover and a pragmatic landlubber. This fiercely independent fisherman casts his traps and his fate to the whims of an itinerant crustacean, the fickle demands of a national market and the unpredictable bounty of a treacherous sea. He admits. "I spend as much time workin' on shore not makin' money as I do out there makin' money." But he'll do it, sometimes well into his 70s, because Maine lobstering is more than an occupation. It's a time-honored way of life.

Year in and year out, he's at the pier before sunrise, loading two 35-gallon bait drums reeking of salted herring onto his boat. Wearing knee-high rubber boots, loose-fitting waterproof overalls and thick cotton gloves, he navigates along the rocky coast through a rolling sea stippled with colorful lobster buoys. If he spots a mackerel gull, he reckons fog's coming in. Superstitious to the core, he won't touch a pork sandwich on board. When he hauls three or four traps consecutively and finds them barren of even spiny sea urchins, he knows in his gut that "someone's been messin' with my traps." On breezy mornings when sunlight dapples the grey-green Atlantic, he confesses that "days like this" compensate for the riskiness of his chosen commerce.

Far from shore and alone in his 26-foot boat, a Maine lobsterman's world resonates with a familiar and comforting symphony. Seagulls caw plaintively, swooping over the bow of the boat as it splashes through choppy swells. The

Marine biologists estimate that 99.9% new-born lobsters die within six weeks, and of the .1% babies that survive the first few months, only 10% might make it through the year.

hydraulic winch grinds noisily, cranking a rope tethered to his trap on the ocean floor. Staccato messages from the ship-to-shore radio punctuate the constant purr of the boat's 292 Chevy motor, and in the distance the bell on a channel marker chimes rhythmically.

When he gets to a trap, he quickly gaffs the rope of his signature buoys which have been painted in a specific combination of colors that he's registered with the state. After hoisting the green wire cage onto the boat's wide gunnel, he measures each potential "keeper" (legally, a lobster measuring between 3-3/16 and 5 inches from eyesocket to end of body) with a ruler and throws back "shorts" and berried lobsters (females coated with eggs). Then, using a metal bander, he slips a thick elastic band around the claws of the keeper which he tosses into a live tank on board. Before cruising to his next buoy, he reloads the bait bag and drops the trap back into the sea. On average, he hauls 200 or more traps daily.

During the balmy summer months when lobsters molt, he averages about one keeper for every third haul. Come fall, when water temperatures plummet and the lobsters are more active, his haul multiplies dramatically and profitably. "You gotta put away for the winter or you won't make it." he says. Occasionally, he's tempted to take home a few choice keepers. "But not that often. I'd rather have the money for it."

Lobster Salad

serves 4

INGREDIENTS

1 pound fresh picked lobster meat, cut into bite-sized pieces

1/4 cup mayonnaise

1/4 cup finely diced celery

TO PREPARE

Combine lobster meat, mayonnaise, and celery and mix well. Store in refrigerator for 2 to 3 hours to allow flavors to blend.

Traditional Maine Lobster Roll

DID YOU KNOW?

🦞 *For the very best lobster rolls, the mayonnaise is mixed with the meat while the meat is still hot. The trick is to use the heat and the steam to flavor the mayonnaise.*

INGREDIENTS

1 frankfurter roll, or your favorite roll

4 ounces (or more) lobster salad

1/4 cup shredded lettuce

TO PREPARE

1. Lightly butter the frankfurter roll and pan grill on both sides until golden brown.
2. Line grilled roll with lettuce and top with lobster salad and serve with potato chips and a dill pickle.

Lobster Salad Plate

makes 1 plate

INGREDIENTS

4 ounces lobster salad

1 avocado, peeled and sliced

1 cup shredded lettuce

1 roasted yellow pepper, sliced

1 roasted red pepper, sliced

TO ROAST PEPPERS

1. Preheat oven to 500 degrees.

2. Place peppers on oiled baking sheet and roast until well blackened

3. Place peppers in a paper bag and seal and let set for 5 minutes. When cool enough to handle, peel, seed and slice.

TO ASSEMBLE THE SALAD PLATE

Place a nest of shredded lettuce in the middle of a chilled plate. Mound lobster salad on the middle of the nest and arrange peppers and avocado around the plate in a decorative fashion.

Ugly Anne's Lobster Stew

This recipe is from Captain Kenneth Young who was a lobsterman in Perkins Cove for more than 40 years. His boat is named *Ugly Anne,* which is how the recipe got its name.

serves 6

INGREDIENTS

1-1/2 pounds fresh picked lobster meat

1/2 pound butter

1 tablespoon dry sherry

1 teaspoon fresh chives

1/2 teaspoon garlic, minced

9 cups milk

3 cups evaporated milk

TO PREPARE

1. Melt butter in skillet, add sherry, chives, garlic, and lobster and cook on low heat for at least 15 minutes.

2. Mix evaporated milk and regular milk in a separate pan and scald.

3. Pour milk mixture into lobster pan and heat through. **Do not boil or cover as stew will curdle.**

4. Serve in warm bowls.

Lobster Gazpacho

serves 8

INGREDIENTS

1 red bell peppers, diced

1 green bell peppers, diced

1 yellow bell peppers, diced

2 cucumbers, peeled, seeded, and diced

1 medium red onions, diced

3 scallions, chopped

1 51-ounce can tomato juice

2-3 drops Tabasco sauce

1-1/2 teaspoons worcestershire sauce

Salt and pepper to taste

1 pound fresh picked lobster meat

TO PREPARE

1. Combine all ingredients except lobster meat and chill well in a plastic or glass container.

2. To serve, place 6 ounces of gazpacho in each bowl and top with a scant quarter-cup fresh chopped lobster meat.

Grilled Lobster Tail Caesar Salad

serves 4

INGREDIENTS

2 lobster tails

1 tablespoon Lobster Oil (see page 16) or olive oil

4 cups Romaine lettuce, rinsed and broken into pieces

4 ounces Caesar dressing (recipe follows)

1/4 cup freshly grated parmesan cheese

8 to 10 croutons

TO PREPARE

1. Split lobster tails, brush lightly with olive oil, or lobster oil and grill meat side down for 4 to 6 minutes.

2. Toss Romaine lettuce with Caesar dressing and cheese and divide onto 4 plates. Sprinkle with croutons.

3. Take lobster tails from the grill and remove meat from the shell. Slice lengthwise and place on top of the salad.

Caesar Dressing

INGREDIENTS

4 egg yolks

2 tablespoons dijon mustard

1-1/2 cups olive oil

1/2 cup Lobster Oil (see page 16)

2 anchovies, mashed

1/3 cup lemon juice

salt and pepper to taste

3/4 cup fresh grated parmesan cheese

1/4 teaspoon Tabasco sauce

1 tablespoon worcestershire sauce

red wine vinegar for thinning

TO PREPARE

1. Whisk the egg yolks and dijon together. Continuing to whisk rapidly, slowly drizzle in the oils until the mixture is thick.

2. Add the anchovies, lemon juice, salt, pepper, parmesan, Tabasco and worcestershire. If mixture is too thick, thin with red wine vinegar until smooth.

3. Cover tightly and keep refrigerated until ready for use.

Lobster Chowder

serves 8

INGREDIENTS

1 quart Lobster Stock (see page 17) or canned clam juice

3 large russet potatoes, peeled and diced

1/4 pound plus 2 tablespoons unsalted butter or Lobster Butter (see page 15)

2 onions peeled and diced

1/4 cup flour

12 to 16 ounces lobster meat

1 quart milk

1 teaspoon salt

1/4 teaspoon freshly ground pepper

TO PREPARE

1. In a medium stock pot, heat lobster stock or clam juice. Add diced potatoes, bring to a boil, lower heat and cook 5 to 7 minutes, or until potatoes are tender.

2. In a separate saute pan, melt 1/4 pound butter, add diced onions and saute until transparent. Add flour and cook, stirring, for 2 to 3 minutes. Add lobster meat to mixture and heat through.

3. Add lobster mixture to potatoes in stock pot.

4. Stir well. Incorporate milk in a slow, steady stream, stirring. Gradually stir in remaining 2 tablespoons of butter.

5. Add salt and pepper and serve in heated bowls.

Lobster Minestrone with Garlic Pesto

serves 6

INGREDIENTS

1/4 cup dried Great Northern beans

1/3 cup dry white wine

16 mussels, cleaned and debearded

1-1/2 to 2 quarts Lobster Stock (see page 17), as needed

2 tablespoons olive oil

2 cloves garlic, minced

1 leek, white part only, diced (wash leek thoroughly after dicing)

1 small onion, diced

1 celery stalk, diced

1/4 cup tomato paste

salt and pepper to taste

1/2 teaspoon dried rosemary

1/2 teaspoon dried thyme

1 slice lemon

1/3 cup Arborio rice (Italian short grain rice)

1-1/2 cups tomato puree

1/2 pound lobster meat

4 teaspoons Roasted Garlic Pesto (see page 32)

TO PREPARE

1. Soak the beans for at least six hours, or overnight.

2. Heat the wine in a medium saucepan over high heat. Add the mussels, cover, and steam until the mussels have opened, 3 to 5 minutes.

3. Strain the mussels and reserve the broth. The mussels may be discarded or reserved for another use.

4. Add enough lobster stock to the mussel broth to equal 2 quarts.

5. Heat the olive oil in a large soup pot. Add the garlic, leek, onion, and celery. Cook over low heat until the onion is translucent.

6. Add the tomato paste, tomato puree, and seasonings. Cook, stirring, about 5 more minutes.

7. Add the reserved stock, lemon slice, rice, and beans. Simmer for about 45 minutes or until the rice and beans are tender.

8. Add the lobster meat to the soup and cook just long enough to heat the lobster.

9. Serve in heated bowls. Garnish each bowl with 1/2 teaspoon Roasted Garlic Pesto.

Lobster & Black Bean Salad

with Cuervo Gold Citronnette

serves 8

INGREDIENTS

4 cups black beans (one pound of dried
beans, cooked, OR 4 cups of canned
beans, rinsed and drained)

1 pound lobster meat, fresh picked and cut
into bite-sized pieces

1 cup diced red peppers

1 cup diced yellow peppers

1 cup sliced scallions

salt and pepper to taste

1 recipe Citronnette (recipe follows)

8 corn tortillas

1 head green leaf lettuce, shredded

8 cilantro sprigs for garnish

TO PREPARE

1. Combine black beans, lobster, peppers, and scallions. Season with salt and pepper.

2. Toss with citronnette and chill for 4 to 6 hours to allow flavors to blend.

3. Place one tortilla on each plate and mound with shredded lettuce. Top with salad mix and garnish with a fresh sprig of cilantro.

Citronnette

INGREDIENTS

1 shot (3 tablespoons) Cuervo Gold tequila, or other good tequila

5 tablespoons lime juice

2 teaspoons chopped fresh cilantro

1 egg white

2/3 cup extra virgin olive oil

TO PREPARE

1. In a small mixing bowl combine the tequila, lime juice, and cilantro.

2. Add egg white and whisk until well incorporated.

3. Gradually whisk in olive oil in a steady stream.

Lobster Bisque

serves 8

INGREDIENTS

10 lobster bodies

2 tablespoons Lobster Oil (see page 16)

2 cloves garlic, chopped

6 shallots, chopped

2 tablespoons brandy

1-1/2 cups white wine

1/4 cup parsley, chopped

2 sprigs fresh thyme

5 cups Lobster Stock (see page 17 or you can substitute with clam juice)

3 tomatoes, quartered

4 tablespoons white rice

salt and pepper to taste

pinch of saffron

pinch of cayenne pepper

3 tablespoons heavy cream

TO PREPARE

1. Rinse lobster and separate the shells from the ribs. Remove the tomalley.

2. In a large pot, heat oil and add garlic and shallots. Saute until transparent and soft.

3. Add the lobster bodies, (shells and ribs) and cook on med-high for about 10 minutes, stirring so as not to scorch.

4. Add the brandy, wine, parsley, thyme and enough stock to cover the bodies. Simmer for 10 to 15 minutes.

5. Remove the bodies and shells from the stock. Cut the rib sections into small pieces. Discard the outer shells and feelers.

6. Return the cut up bodies to the liquid and add the remaining stock, tomatoes, rice, and salt and pepper. Simmer mixture for 30 minutes, or until rice is tender.

7. Strain the soup through a fine sieve, pushing down on all the ingredients to extract all the juices.

8. Put the soup into into a pot and add the saffron, cayenne pepper, and cream. Simmer for 5 minutes and adjust the seasonings.

Our Favorite House Salad

serves 4

INGREDIENTS

8 cups baby green lettuces, torn into bite-sized pieces

1 cup fresh mango, diced

3 ounces Maytag bleu cheese, crumbled

1/3 cup walnut halves, toasted

1/3 cup sun-dried cranberries

4 ounces fresh picked lobster meat

1/2 cup walnut vinaigrette

1. Toss lettuces, mango, bleu cheese, walnuts, and sun-dried cranberries in a large salad bowl. Drizzle with the dressing just before serving.

WALNUT VINAIGRETTE

yields 1 cup

3/4 cup walnut oil

1/4 cup balsamic vinegar

1 egg white

salt and pepper to taste

2 teaspoons dried herbes de Provence

1. In a small stainless steel bowl, gradually whisk oil into vinegar.
2. Whisk in egg white, salt, pepper, and herbs.

Maine Plates

Lobster Legends

Maine lobstermen put out to sea with a homespun code of salty suspicions. They won't eat walnuts on board or leave a hatch cover upside down. They hate the color blue and never utter the word p-i-g. Bringing a woman along to check traps or sticking a knife in a wooden deck is considered downright chancy. "Nobody believes this stuff," they admit. "We just don't do it."

Over the centuries lobstering has inspired countless yarns along Maine's serpentine shoreline. Old timers still debate the precise location of "Stretcher's Cove," so named for a secluded inlet where rogue fishermen anchored ever-so-briefly to pull and elongate lobster tails to "keeper" size.

Others recall when they hid their school lunch pails behind a pine tree or beneath a rock. They were ashamed to eat yet another lobster sandwich which the gentry's children labeled "poor man's food."

There are sentimental stories of how lobstering inspired romance. One day a smitten gal walked to the town pier, hoping to greet the man of her dreams as his boat chugged into port. When she caught him catnapping in his dory and noticed that his hands were red and sore, she ran home to get Cornhusker's Lotion. Her loving ministrations to his chapped hands kindled his affections, and they married within the year.

One dark and stormy night during Prohibition, a rum-runner ran aground among the rocks near Ogunquit. Word quickly spread about the contents of the three-gallon barrels bobbing in the white-capped waters. Locals realized that the revenuers would impound the valuable flotsam anyway, so they quickly commandeered every boat in town and steamed out to hoist the hooch for themselves. It was, by all accounts, a most spirited summer along the coast.

Records indicate that in 1840 lobsters generally sold for 2 cents each.

"Tender lobster" means one thing to a gourmet. To thrifty Maine housewives, it translates to money in the sugarbowl. When scant hauls pinched their household budgets, their husbands plied the grocer with "shorts" to pay for fresh milk and eggs. Indeed, there's hardly a village along the north Atlantic seaboard that at one time or another hasn't relied on lobsters to plump the local economy. Only one, however, came to be known as the "Lobster Plug Capital of the World."

Since lobsters are cantankerous and cannibalistic in captivity, something was needed to immobilize their deadly crusher claws. The ingenious Acadians in West Pubnico rose to that challenge a century ago, whittling by hand individual 1-1/4-inch-long by half-inch-wide pegs from the soft pine that grew abundantly in their backyards. Once that peg was inserted into the chela, lobster longevity was generally ensured until they ended up in serious hot water.

The growing demand for live lobster escalated the need for pegs and lined West Pubnico's pockets. Housewives sold them to dealers (a bag of 1,000 yielded 50 cents) or bartered them to purchase cloth, thread, flour and molasses. School boys traded bags of pegs for candy and cigarettes. Local doctors accepted them in lieu of cash. Sitting around the fire on long winter nights, almost everyone did their whittle thing. By the late 1960s, it's estimated that more than 20 million pegs were being carved by hand annually in this village of 2,000.

The thriving cottage industry ground to a halt in the next decade when the wheels of progress rolled into town. Newly-built factories replaced human hands in manufacturing the wooden pegs. Then, in 1984, the lobster industry changed over to thick elastic bands to secure the claws. Today, the knives and leather thumb protectors used to whittle these pegs gather dust on closet shelves. West Pubnico's heyday as the lobster plug capital of the world is history.

Bouillabaisse

This is a traditional Bouillabaisse broth with New England shellfish and fish. The flavor in the stock is from the mussels and clams rather than fish racks. It is served with rouille and toasted french bread.

serves 8

INGREDIENTS

2 tablespoons fennel seed, or 1 fennel bulb, chopped

1/2 cup extra-virgin olive oil

3 leeks, white part only, coarsely chopped

2 large onions, coarsely chopped

8 cloves of garlic, unpeeled, cut in half

4 stalks of celery, chopped

6 sprigs of parsley

10 whole black peppercorns

2 bay leaves

1 tablespoon dried rosemary

2 pinches saffron

1 tablespoon dried thyme

salt to taste

freshly ground pepper to taste

1/2 cup tomato paste

1 28-ounce can Italian plum tomatoes

grated zest of 1/2 orange

2 pounds mussels, cleaned, not debearded

1 pound littleneck clams, cleaned

8 cups water

4 cups dry white wine

1 pound swordfish, cut into 8 portions

1 pound halibut, cut into 8 portions

8 lobster tails, split in half

8 jumbo shrimp

8 large sea scallops

16 littleneck clams

16 mussels, cleaned and debearded

TO PREPARE

1. In a large stockpot, over medium heat, saute fennel seed or fennel bulb in olive oil until fragrant, about 2 minutes.

2. Add leeks, onion, garlic and celery, and saute until vegetables are softened, about 10 minutes.

3. Add to the stockpot the herbs and seasonings, tomato paste, tomatoes, and orange zest, mixing well.

4. To the pot now add 2 pounds of mussels and one pound of clams, the water and the wine.

5. Cover the pot and bring to a boil for 10 minutes. Reduce heat and simmer uncovered for 45 minutes to an hour.

6. Strain the broth through a sieve, extracting as much of the vegetable juices as possible.

7. Return the stock to the pot and bring back to heat.

8. Add the fish and remaining shellfish, and gently simmer until clams and mussels open.

9. Divide seafood among 8 heated bowls, add broth and serve with french bread and rouille.

Rouille

makes approximately 1 cup

INGREDIENTS

1/2 cup bread crumbs, soaked in 1 cup water

4 cloves garlic, peeled

1/2 tablespoon red pepper flakes

1/4 cup olive oil

2 drops Tabasco sauce

1 tablespoon paprika

3–4 spoonfuls of Bouillabaisse broth

TO PREPARE

1. Strain the bread crumbs in a towel and squeeze out extra moisture.

2. In work bowl of food processor, fitted with knife blade, combine all ingredients except broth.

3. Process to a smooth paste and gradually add broth. The rouille should be the consistency of mayonnaise.

DID YOU KNOW?

The bouillabaisse can be served with any type of firm flesh fish, more or less seafood, as one desires.

The broth is great adding just cooked pasta and a little seafood to it.

The rouille is best spread on bread and dipped into the broth.

The rouille is also a great accompaniment to grilled or pan roasted fish.

Lobster Benedict

serves 4

INGREDIENTS

8 ounces fresh picked lobster meat

1 tablespoon melted butter

4 English Muffins, split and toasted

8 eggs, poached

1 cup Hollandaise Sauce (recipe follows)

TO PREPARE

1. Saute lobster meat in melted butter until well heated, being sure not to overcook.
2. Divide muffins on four plates and top each with 1 ounce of lobster meat. Place poached egg on top of each muffin and top with hollandaise.

TO POACH EGGS:

1 quart water

3 tablespoons white vinegar

1. Bring water to a rolling boil.
2. Break eggs one at a time gently into the water. Reduce heat and let eggs steep until whites are firm. Remove eggs with a slotted spoon and drain.

DID YOU KNOW?

🦞 *Eggs can be poached in advanced and reheated for 30 seconds in boiling water. Salt will break down the white and should not be used.*

Hollandaise Sauce

INGREDIENTS

3 egg yolks

1 tablespoon water

1/2 pound butter, melted and still warm

3 tablespoons fresh lemon juice

salt and pepper to taste

TO PREPARE

1. In a food processor fitted with the knife blade, beat the egg yolks and water for 30 seconds. With the machine running, add the melted butter in a slow steady stream.

2. Add the lemon juice, salt and pepper and process just to blend.

Lobster Lasagne with Fresh Asparagus

serves 8

INGREDIENTS

2 pounds asparagus, trimmed

3 tablespoons olive oil

salt and pepper to taste

6 8-inch square sheets no-boil lasagne

4 tablespoons (1/2 stick) butter

1/4 cup flour

2 cups chicken stock

12 ounces Brie cheese, peeled and chopped

1/4 cup sherry

12 ounces fresh picked lobster meat

1 pound tomatoes, sliced

1 1/3 cups freshly grated parmesan cheese

TO PREPARE

1. Preheat oven to 500 degrees.
2. In a shallow baking pan toss the asparagus with olive oil, coating them well. Roast them in the preheated oven for 5 to 10 minutes until they are crisp, but tender. Sprinkle with salt and pepper and let cool. Cut into 2 inch pieces and reserve. Reduce oven to 400 degrees.
3. In a large bowl of cold water let the lasagne sheets soak for 15 minutes to soften.

4. In a sauce pan melt the butter and then add the flour and cook over low heat, stirring for 3 minutes. Add the chicken stock in a slow, steady stream and whisk until thickened. Add one-third of the Brie and whisk until melted and smooth. Repeat the process until all the Brie is used and then add the sherry and adjust the seasonings. Set aside.

TO ASSEMBLE

1. Drain lasagne sheets and arrange one sheet in each of two well greased 8-inch square baking pans.

2. Spread a thin layer of sauce (about 1/2 cup) over each lasagne. Top with one-quarter of the amounts of the asparagus, tomato slices, and lobster. Sprinkle with parmesan cheese. Place another sheet of lasagne in each pan, and repeat the process. Top each pan with a third sheet of lasagne, and the remaining sauce and cheese.

3. Bake lasagne in a 400 degree oven for 20 to 30 minutes or until golden brown and bubbling. Remove from oven and let stand for 10 minutes before serving.

Linguini with Lobster and Braised Garlic

serves 6 to 8 as a first course; 4 to 6 as a main course

INGREDIENTS

1 pound linguini, cooked and drained

1/4 cup extra virgin olive oil

8 large garlic cloves, cut into 1/4 inch dice

2 pounds lobster meat, fresh picked and cut into bite-sized pieces

6 teaspoons good quality balsamic vinegar

1/4 cup fresh basil, chopped

TO PREPARE

1. Prepare linguini according to instructions on package, rinse and drain.
2. In a heavy-bottomed skillet heat olive oil and add the garlic. Lower heat and cover and cook for 5 minutes. Uncover and continue to cook for 10 minutes or until garlic is lightly colored.
3. Add the lobster meat to the garlic and oil and heat through.
4. Toss drained linguini with lobster and garlic. Add balsamic vinegar and half the chopped basil and toss well.
5. Garnish with remaining basil and serve.

Lobster Risotto

serves 8

INGREDIENTS

1/2 cup diced shallots

2 cloves garlic, diced

1 tablespoon olive oil

2 cups Arborio rice (Italian short grain rice)

1 cup dry white wine

5 cups chicken broth, heated

1 cup lobster stock or bottled clam juice, heated

1 pound fresh picked lobster meat, coarsely chopped

1 can (6 to 8) artichoke hearts, sliced

1 cup minced sun-dried tomatoes

1/4 cup fresh parsley chopped

TO PREPARE

1. In a large pot saute shallots and garlic in olive oil until softened.
2. Over medium heat, add rice and stir to coat with oil. Add the wine and stir until absorbed. Combine the chicken broth and lobster stock and add the warm broth 1 cup at a time until the rice is tender. This should take about 30 minutes.
3. Just before the rice is done, add the lobster meat, artichoke hearts, sun-dried tomatoes, and parsley. Mix well. Serve immediately.

DID YOU KNOW?

When cooking arborio rice always allow each cup of liquid to become absorbed before adding the next cup.

It is always 3 to 3-1/2 cups liquid to 1 cup rice.

Never add grated cheese to seafood risotto.

Lobster & Chicken Gumbo

serves 8

INGREDIENTS

1 4-pound chicken

1-1/2 quarts chicken stock (canned is fine)

1/2 pound (4 links) hot Italian sausage

1 tablespoon olive oil

2 cups celery, diced

1-1/2 cups green peppers, diced

2 cups yellow onions, diced

6 scallions, diced

1/2 pound mushrooms, quartered

1 pound asparagus, cut into bite-sized pieces

1 clove garlic, minced

2 tablespoons chili powder

3 tablespoons oregano

3 tablespoons cumin

1/2 teaspoon cayenne pepper

1 tablespoon red pepper flakes

1 28-ounce can whole tomatoes in juice

1 28-ounce can tomato puree

3 tablespoons granulated sugar

1 pound fresh lobster meat, cut into bite-sized pieces

TO PREPARE

1. Put chicken in a large pot, add stock, cover and bring to a boil. Reduce heat to simmer and cook approximately 25 to 30 minutes, until chicken is fully cooked.

2. In a large heavy-bottomed saucepan add the olive oil and sausage. Pierce sausage with a fork and cook until sausage is cooked and well browned.

3. Remove sausage from pan and let cool. When the sausage is cool enough to handle, slice on the diagonal 1/4-inch thick.

4. Add all the vegetables and seasonings to the olive oil and sausage fat and saute until onions are transparent and vegetables are soft.

5. Add whole tomatoes and their juice and the tomato puree and stir well and continue to cook.

6. When chicken is cool enough to handle, pick meat and cut into bite-sized pieces. Add the chicken, sausage, and sugar to the tomato and vegetable mixture. Continue to simmer for another 1/2 hour.

7. When ready to serve, add the lobster meat, allowing it to heat through and serve with rice.

Lobster Ravioli Americaine

serves 8

INGREDIENTS

1 pound Pasta Dough (see next page)

2 1-1/2 pound Maine Boiled Lobsters (see page 14)

2 tablespoons butter

1 carrot, diced

1 celery stalk, diced

1 small onion, diced

1 shallot, minced

1 clove garlic, minced

3 tablespoons brandy

1 cup dry white wine

2 cups water

2 teaspoons tomato paste

3-1/2 cups heavy cream

1/2 pound scallops

1/4 pound fillet of sole, chopped

2 eggs

TO PREPARE

1. Prepare pasta dough and set aside.

2. Remove lobster meat from shells and set aside. Break shells into small pieces and reserve.

3. Prepare the sauce: Melt the butter in a large pot over low heat. Add the carrot, celery, onion, shallot, and garlic. Cover the pot and cook for about 10 minutes or until softened, stirring occasionally. Do not brown.

4. Add the lobster shells to the vegetable mixture. Cook, uncovered, for 2 minutes. Add the brandy and ignite. When the flame dies down, add the wine and stir well. Add the water and tomato paste. Simmer, partially covered, for 30 minutes.

5. Add 2 cups of the cream and simmer until thickened, about 30 minutes. While sauce is thickening, prepare the filling.

6. To prepare the filling: Cut 8 slices from the reserved lobster meat and set aside for garnish. Dice the remaining lobster meat and set aside.

7. Puree the scallops and sole in food processor fitted with the knife blade for about 1 minute. Add the eggs and process for 30 seconds. Place the work bowl in the freezer and chill for 30 seconds.

8. Add the diced lobster meat to the work bowl and return the bowl to the food processor. Turn on machine and slowly pour in 1-1/2 cups of chilled cream. Process for 30 seconds.

9. To assemble the ravioli: Using a pasta machine, roll dough into pairs of sheets of approximately the same size. The size of the matching sheets is not as important as the thickness. The dough should be as thin as possible without tearing. Experiment with a small piece of dough before rolling the rest of it. Be sure to flour the rollers of the machine to prevent sticking.

10. Mound 2 tablespoons of the seafood mixture in rows on one sheet of dough, 2 inches apart, with a 1-inch border along the edges of the sheet. Lightly brush the exposed dough with water and lay a second sheet over the first.

11. Press down around the mounds of filling to seal. Using a knife or pastry cutter, cut down the center of the borders that separate the mounds of filling.

12. Allow ravioli to rest for up to an hour. To cook, poach gently for 5 to 10 minutes, and serve with sauce.

PASTA DOUGH

makes 1 pound

INGREDIENTS

3 cups flour

4 large eggs

1 teaspoon salt

1 tablespoon olive oil

TO PREPARE

1. In the bowl of an electric mixer with a paddle attachment, combine the dry ingredients.

2. Add the eggs and oil and mix at low speed until small bits of dough form, in about 30 seconds.

3. Replace the paddle with a dough hook. Mix the dough until it forms a ball, about 5 minutes.

4. Place the dough on a flat surface dusted with flour and knead for 5 to 10 minutes, until it is smooth and elastic.

5. Form the dough into a ball and place it in a bowl. Cover and allow to rest for 30 minutes and up to 2 hours.

Lobsters on the Grill

serves 4

INGREDIENTS

4 1 to 2 pound live lobsters

1/4 pound butter, melted

1 lemon, cut into wedges

TO PREPARE

1. Boil lobsters for 5 minutes, remove from pot and drain.
2. Lightly crack claws and split tails on rib side so as to let the smoke from the grill flavor the meat.
3. Place lobsters on a medium-hot grill. Cook for 8 to 10 minutes, turning occasionally to avoid burning the shells.
4. Serve with melted butter and lemon wedges.

Lobster Cassoulet

serves 8

INGREDIENTS

1 pound dried Great Northern beans

1/8 pound (1/3 cup) dried cranberry beans

1/8 pound (1/3 cup) dried red kidney beans

1/8 pound (1/3 cup) dried black beans

1 sprig fresh thyme

1 bay leaf

2 cloves garlic, peeled and chopped

1 quart Lobster Stock (see page 17)

1/8 cup olive oil

1/2 cup diced onions

1/2 cup finely diced carrots

1/2 cup diced bacon

4 cloves garlic, minced

1 pound plum tomatoes, peeled, seeded, and chopped

1 tablespoon dried thyme

1 pound lobster meat, coarsely chopped

2 cups fresh bread crumbs

TO PREPARE

1. Soak the beans for at least 6 hours, or overnight. Soak the black beans separately from the rest.

2. Cook the beans in the herbs, garlic, and stock until tender, about 30 minutes.

3. In a large pot over low heat, heat the olive oil and saute the onions, carrots, bacon, and garlic until the onions are translucent.

4. Add the tomatoes and thyme, and continue to cook for about 5 minutes.

5. Add the beans to the vegetable mixture. Cook for another 10 minutes. Add lobster and remove from heat.

6. Preheat oven to 375 degrees. Ladle cassoulet into oven-proof bowls and top with bread crumbs. Bake until browned, about 10 minutes.

Steamed Lobster

INGREDIENTS

1 quart salted tap water or sea water

6 1-1/2 pound lobsters

12 quart pot with lid

TO PREPARE

1. Place about 1 inch of salted or sea water in a large stock pot. Bring to a boil.
2. Remove elastic bands from lobsters and place head first into the pot.
3. Cover the pot and return to a boil.
4. Steam on high for 10 to 12 minutes, depending on the hardness of the shell. Lobsters should be done when a tentacle is easily snapped.
5. Remove pot from burner and allow to steep for 3 to 4 minutes.
6. Serve with drawn butter.

Drawn Butter

1 pound unsalted butter

TO PREPARE

1. Melt butter on low heat.
2. Skim foam from top of butter. Do not stir.
3. Ladle into 2 ounce cups carefully, as not to stir up the solids on the bottom of the pot.

DID YOU KNOW?

🦞 *It takes four 1 pound lobsters to make one pound of picked meat.*

🦞 *It takes 7 years for a lobster to reach 1 pound.*

🦞 *Lobsters shed their shells once a year, usually in early summer*

🦞 *It takes six 1 pound shedders to get 1 pound of meat.*

🦞 *Soft shelled lobsters cook much more quickly than hard shelled.*

Oven Roasted Lobster

with fresh herb and pistachio sauce

serves 4 for lunch or 2 for dinner

INGREDIENTS

4 1 to 2 pound live Maine Lobsters

2 tablespoons Lobster Oil (see page 16)

1/2 cup shelled pistachios, coarsely chopped

1 large shallot, finely chopped

2 tablespoons chopped fresh basil

1 teaspoon chopped fresh mint

1 teaspoon chopped fresh oregano

1/4 cup cognac

3 tablespoons dry sherry

TO PREPARE

1. Preheat oven to 400 degrees.

2. Boil lobsters for 5 minutes. Remove from pot and drain.

3. When each lobster is cool enough to handle, separate the claws and knuckles from the body. Pick the meat from the claws and knuckles, trying to leave it as whole as possible.

4. Split the lobster body in half and remove the head sac. Rinse lobster under cold running water to clean. Drain, meat side down.

5. Put roasting pan with lobster oil into the preheated oven for 3 minutes. Add lobster body, meat side down, and roast for 10 minutes.

6. Remove pan from oven, add the pistachios, shallot, claw and knuckle meat and return to oven for 5 more minutes.

7. Remove pan from oven and place on stove top set on high heat. Remove lobster bodies and set aside on heated foil-tented plates to keep warm. Add cognac to pan and ignite. When flame has gone out, add sherry.

8. Reduce heat to medium, add herbs and butter, 1 tablespoon at a time. When all the butter has been added, fill lobster cavities with meat and nut mixture and drizzle all the sauce over the lobsters.

Lobster Thermidor

serves 4

INGREDIENTS

4 1-1/2 pound lobsters

8 tablespoons unsalted butter

2 shallots, minced

2 cloves garlic, minced

4 ounces fresh Maine crabmeat

4 ounces baby Maine shrimp

4 ounces bay scallops

1 cup mushrooms, sliced

1/2 cup soft bread crumbs

1 tablespoon worcestershire sauce

1/4 teaspoon Tabasco sauce

salt and pepper to taste

1 tablespoon parsley, chopped

3/4 cup dry sherry

1/4 cup brandy

1-1/2 cups heavy cream

4 egg yolks, lightly beaten

1/2 cup freshly grated parmesan cheese

paprika

TO PREPARE

1. Bring a large pot of water to a boil and plunge lobsters head first into the pot and boil for 8 to 10 minutes. Lobsters should be bright red and the tentacle should be snapped easily. Remove and set aside until they are cool enough to handle.

2. Break off the claws and knuckles from the lobster bodies and pick the meat from the shells.

3. With the lobster on its back, cut it down the middle and remove the stomach, intestinal vein, and head sac. Cut the thin under shell from the tail section and remove the meat. Chop all the reserved lobster meat.

4. Preheat oven to 350 degrees.

5. Heat 1/2 the butter in a large saute pan. Add the garlic and shallots and cook until soft. Add the lobster meat, crabmeat, scallops, shrimp, mushrooms, bread crumbs, worcestershire, Tabasco, salt and pepper, parsley, sherry, brandy, and heavy cream and heat until it just starts to boil.

6. Add the egg yolks and cook until the mixture has thickened. (3 to 5 minutes)

7. When mixture has cooled slightly, fill the reserved lobster shells. Sprinkle with parmesan cheese, dot with remaining butter and sprinkle with paprika.

8. Put lobsters in baking dish and place in preheated oven for 15 minutes.

Spaghetti with Lobster & Clams in foil

serves 8

INGREDIENTS

3-1/2 tablespoons olive oil

2 cloves garlic, chopped

1 teaspoon dried chili pepper flakes

24 hard neck Maine clams

1 cup white wine

1 14-ounce can whole tomatoes in juice, chopped

salt and pepper to taste

2 tablespoons parsley, chopped

1 pound spaghetti

1 pound fresh picked lobster meat, chopped

TO PREPARE

1. Preheat oven to 425 degrees.
2. Heat the oil in a large pot. Add the garlic, pepper flakes, clams, and white wine and cook until the clams start to open.
3. Add the tomatoes and their juice, parsley, and salt and pepper. Simmer for 5 more minutes.
4. Cook the pasta for half the allotted time on the package and drain.
5. Toss the pasta with the sauce and lobster.
6. Have a double layer of foil ready on a baking sheet. Put the spaghetti mixture in the center of the foil and fold the foil tightly so that no steam will escape.
7. Bake in the oven for 8 to 10 minutes.
8. Place foil on a large platter and open at the table.

Lobster Stuffed Pasta Shells

serves 6

INGREDIENTS

2 tablespoons butter

2 tablespoons shallots, minced

3/4 cup white wine

12 ounces shiitake mushrooms, sliced

1 tablespoon parsley, chopped

1 tablespoon basil, chopped

9 ounces mascarpone cheese

1 pound fresh picked lobster meat

1/2 cup fresh bread crumbs

1 box jumbo pasta shells, cooked according to the package directions

TO PREPARE

1. Saute shallots in butter until transparent. Add the white wine and reduce by one half.

2. When the wine is reduced by one half, add the mushrooms, parsley, and basil and saute until the mushrooms are tender.

3. Add the mascarpone cheese and lobster to the mushroom mixture and heat through.

4. Add the bread crumbs slowly to the mixture to tighten. Note that you might not need all the bread crumbs. When cool enough to handle, stuff into the pasta shells. Set aside until ready for service.

5. When ready to serve, place in a shallow baking dish with a couple of tablespoons of water and cover with foil. Heat in a 350 degree oven for 7 to 10 minutes. Serve with Boursin Cream (recipe follows).

BOURSIN CREAM

1 quart heavy cream

4 ounces boursin cheese

1. To 1 quart of heavy cream, add 4 ounces of boursin cheese and heat, stirring to blend well.

Maine Downeast Clambake

This is probably the first way lobsters and clams were eaten along the Maine coast and it's still the preferred choice for many Mainers who want to celebrate during the summer months. Although the methods change somewhat from one "Bake master" to another, the results are usually the same. If you haven't gotten a mouthful of sand or grit, then the bake just "wasn't like it used to be." The one area in which all "Bake masters" differ is how long the bake cooks from start to finish, some saying it takes five beers while others say it is as many as seven or eight before the bake should be uncovered. You decide how many beers you want, just keep in mind the more beer you have, the better the sand tastes. We would recommend one lobster, about a pound of clams, two or three potatoes, if they're small, one onion, and one hot dog per person. But if your guests have large appetites, adjust the amounts accordingly.

Your Favorite Chowder	Lobsters
Steamer (soft shell) Clams	Red Potatoes
Yellow Onions	Corn on the Cob
Hot Dogs	Corn Muffins or your favorite rolls

Start by digging a hole, on the beach, about 3 feet wide by 3 feet deep and about 6 feet in length. Next, you want to gather any drift wood that looks dry enough to burn. Throw all the wood into the hole and get a rip-snorting fire burning. While the fire is burning, gather as many heavy rocks as you will need to line the bottom of the hole. When the fire turns to a red glow, throw all the rocks on the top of the coals. When the flame goes out, cover the rocks with at least one bushel of fresh cut seaweed (rock weed). That should get a nice steam going. On top of the seaweed (rock weed) put corn, onions potatoes, lobster, hot dogs and top that with the steamers. Place another bushel of fresh seaweed (rock weed) on top of the whole thing. Spray the seaweed (rock weed) with some salt water and let it steam 45 minutes to an hour. Remove a test onion, it should be soft, and the clam shells should be open. (Some people cover everything with a piece of canvas to ensure proper cooking. Remember to shorten your cooking time if you do.) Serve the chowder when everyone starts to ask when the bake is going to be ready and when it's time to uncover the bake, just let everyone serve themselves.

Clambake on the Range

Your Favorite Chowder

1 can of beer

Lobster

Clams

Corn

Red Potatoes, par boiled

Corn Muffins

1. Serve bowls of your favorite chowder when you start to cook your clambake on the range.
2. Add 1(12-ounce) can of beer to a large steamer or soup pot. Add the corn, lobsters, clams, and potatoes in that order. Cover, and bring to a boil. Let it all steam for 15 minutes or until the clams are opened and the lobsters are bright red. Serve with corn muffins.

Maine's Best Clambake(s)

The simplest way to enjoy a Maine or Downeast Clambake is to have a professional "Bake Master" cater the affair. The two best whom we know of, both having catered for Presidents of the United States, are Bill Fosters Downeast Clambakes in York, Maine (207-363-3255) or Cape-Port Caterers in Kennebunkport, Maine (207-967-5457).

Baked Stuffed Lobster

serves 6

INGREDIENTS

6 1-1/2 pound Maine Lobsters

6 cups Seafood Stuffing (see next page)

TO PREPARE

1. Preheat oven to 450 degrees.
2. To kill lobsters, insert the tip of a large knife between the eyes and split the lobster lengthwise Discard the small, tough sac near the eyes of each lobster. Remove the coral and livers and discard. Twist off the claws and set aside.
3. Divide the seafood stuffing evenly among the lobsters. Place on sheet pans and bake for 15 to 20 minutes in the oven.
4. Bring a pot of water to a boil and boil claws for 8 to 10 minutes. (Claws could be baked with the stuffed bodies, but we feel for best results, they should be boiled.)

Lobster Seafood Stuffing

stuffing for 6 to 8 lobsters, depending on their size

INGREDIENTS

1/2 pound butter, or Lobster Butter (see page 15)

1/2 cup finely chopped shallot

6 stalks celery, trimmed and diced

1/4 cup chopped parsley

1/2 teaspoon thyme

1/4 teaspoon salt

6 twists peppermill

1/2 pound fresh Maine crabmeat

1/2 pound baby Maine shrimp, peeled

1/2 pound small bay scallops

1-1/2 pounds (12 cups) crushed Ritz crackers

1 cup dry sherry

TO PREPARE

1. Saute shallot and celery in butter or lobster butter until transparent. Add herbs and seafood and continue to cook until seafood is just cooked through, about 10 minutes.

2. Add the Ritz crackers and mix thoroughly, adding the sherry at the end. Makes about 12 cups of stuffing or enough to stuff 6 to 8 lobsters, depending on size.

Suggested Holiday Menus

NEW YEAR'S DAY BRUNCH BUFFET

Bloody Marys and Mimosas

Lobster Quiche with Mascarpone Cheese (page 38)

Lobster Hash (page 41)

Lobster Benedict (page 68)

Standing Rib Roast

Hash Brown Potatoes

Our Favorite House Salad (page 59)

Crusty Sourdough Bread

Frozen White Chocolate Mousse with Strawberries soaked in Kirsch

CHRISTMAS EVE OPEN HOUSE

Egg Nog or Raspberry Champagne Punch

Ugly Anne's Lobster Stew (page 50)

Maple Sugar Glazed Ham

Lobster Lasagne with Fresh Asparagus (page 70)

Tourtiére (Canadian Pork Pie)

Grilled Lobster Tail Caesar Salad (page 52)

French Baguettes with Sweet Butter

Yuletide Fruit Trifle

Lobster-shaped Sugar Cookies